Hikes to Peaks & Vistas

in Shenandoah National Park

Table of Contents

Introduction 2
Map of Shenandoah National Park 4
Leave No Trace/Special Alerts 5
Compton Peak 6
Pass Mountain 8
Marys Rock 10
Stony Man Mountain 12
Hawksbill Mountain 14
Hightop Mountain 16
Loft Mountain (Frazier Discovery Trail) 18
Chimney Rock 20
Turk Mountain 22
If You Want More 24
Hike Statistics . . . . Back Cover

Introduction

Yes, the views from Skyline Drive and its overlooks are truly superb. But perhaps you're one of the many who'd like to hike to a view, away from the cars and the Drive. Then this guide is for you: directions for nine hikes in Shenandoah National Park to peaks and high places with outstanding vistas.

Although these hikes involve a climb, it's often a minimal one—only 340 feet to the top of Stony Man, for example, a mountain prominent in park history, with a view to the west that is surely among the finest in the park. And because the hikes described in the guide start from Skyline Drive, which winds along the crest of the Blue Ridge Mountains, you're starting off **close** to the peaks and high places; in fact, the longest round-trip hike in the guide is only 3.4 miles and the shortest is a mere 1.3!

As you hike to a peak, you'll experience so much of the world of Shenandoah. You'll walk through forest. You'll pass rocks, flowers, and wildlife. On many of the hikes—the Frazier Discovery Trail on Loft Mountain is one—you'll use the very same paths walked by the families who once lived in these mountains. When you reach the observation platform on Hawksbill, you'll have climbed to the tallest peak in the park. When you hike to Marys Rock and Chimney Rock, you'll witness nature's renewal after fire. When you hike on Pass Mountain or Turk Mountain or on the Riprap Trail to Chimney Rock, you'll be in a federally designated wilderness area. And when you stand on the rocks atop any peak, from the greenstone of Compton Peak in the north to the quartzite of Turk Mountain in the south, you'll look out over vistas that can stun you into silence.

Stay awhile! Such moments are precious.

What to bring: necessary
- ✓ This booklet.
- ✓ Comfortable walking shoes.
- ✓ Hat, gloves, and jacket fitting the season.
- ✓ Drinking water. (Don't drink the water from springs or streams unless you boil or purify it.)

What to bring: helpful but optional
- ✓ A first aid kit.
- ✓ Fun things like binoculars, camera, field guides, magnifier, sketch pad.

Directions
- ✓ **Mile** is your starting point on Skyline Drive. A milepost on the west side of the Drive marks each mile.
- ✓ **AT** is the Appalachian Trail—the National Scenic Trail which stretches over 2,100 miles between Baxter Peak on Katahdin in Maine and Springer Mountain in Georgia.
- ✓ **Circuit hike** means that the trail loops around to the starting point; you don't retrace your steps to return.
- ✓ **Round-trip hike** means that you turn around and retrace your steps to return.
- ✓ A **switchback** is a sharp turn on a trail—sometimes as sharp as a close U turn.

Trail Markers
- ✓ **Trailposts** are concrete posts at the start of many trails and at all trail intersections. A metal band at the top of the post gives trail names and distances. It's wise to read all four sides of the metal band, to be sure of your direction.
- ✓ **Blazes** are paint marks 2" x 6" on trees or rocks: white blazes for the Appalachian Trail, blue for other hiking trails, and yellow for horse trails (which hikers may also use, but horses have the right of way). A **double blaze** (one blaze above another) indicates a sharp turn.

Leave No Trace

Everyone who wishes to protect the natural world we live in and practice good environmental ethics is committed to Leave No Trace—seven principles which help you to minimize your impact on the environment. As you hike the trails in the park, experiencing and discovering, remember these seven principles.

1. Plan ahead and prepare.
2. Travel and camp on durable surfaces.
3. Dispose of waste properly.
4. Leave what you find.
5. Minimize campfire impacts.
   (campfires prohibited in Shenandoah's backcountry)
6. Respect wildlife.
7. Be considerate of other visitors.

Special Alerts

- As you hike, please follow park regulations and **Leave No Trace Principle #4**. Leave wildflowers, trees, animals, rocks, artifacts, and cultural sites as they are so that those who come after you can enjoy them, too.

- Be careful as you walk, stand, or sit on the rocks at the viewing spots. Hawksbill summit has a viewing platform with a protective wall around it, but the others don't, and all the peaks and high places look out over steep drops. Also, rocks are very slippery when wet.

- **Park Emergency Number: (800) 732-0911**

Compton Peak

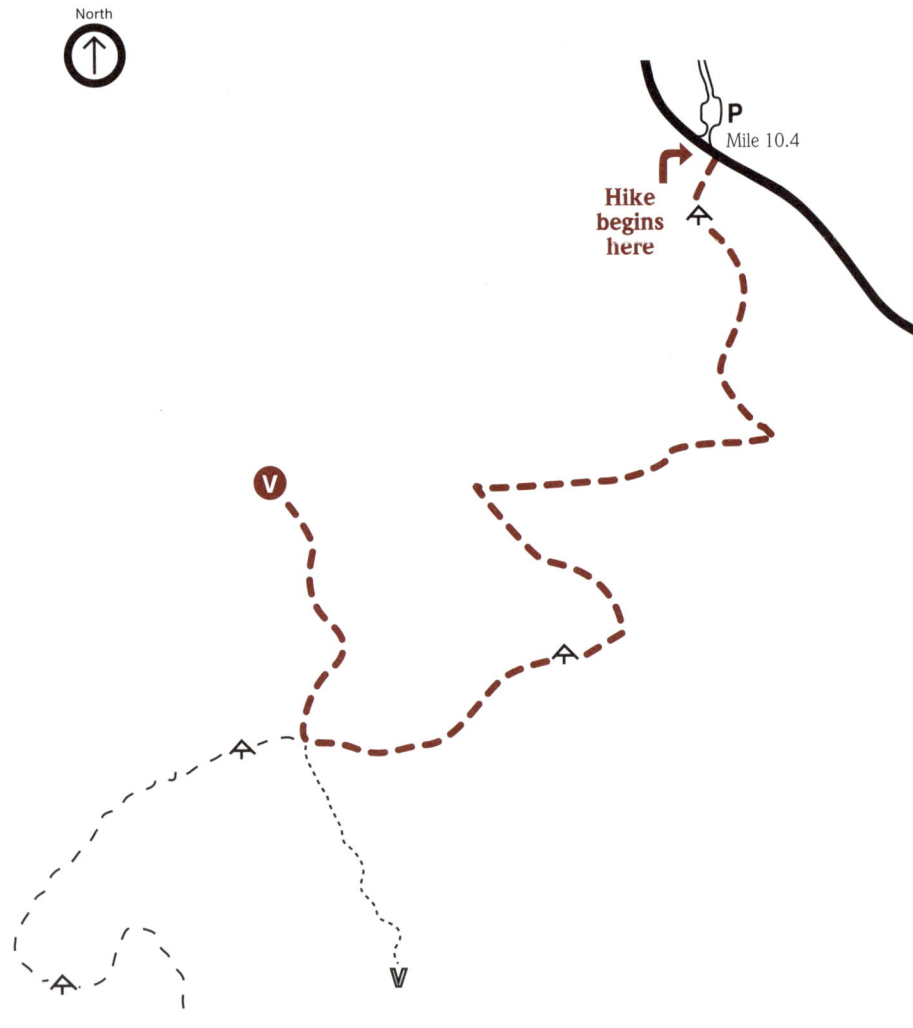

Compton Peak
Skyline Drive access: mile 10.4

It's just 1 mile uphill on this, the northernmost hike in this guide, a **round-trip hike** of **2 miles**. The trail, rocky in spots, is not too difficult, and the spectacular view from the top includes a section of Skyline Drive.

Park at the Compton Gap parking area at mile 10.4, on the east side of Skyline Drive. The trailpost at the entrance to the parking area doesn't mention Compton Peak, but it's right above you! Cross the Drive to the west side and start walking on the AT going south, following the white blazes. You'll move gradually uphill into dense shade when foliage is out, mostly from oak, beech, locust, sassafras, and other hardwoods. You'll see many other trees, including young chestnuts and striped maples, and in summer you're likely to have dense brush and grass on both sides. In season, wildflowers brighten the trail, including wild roses, wild columbine, hawkweed, purple flowering raspberry, long-leaved bluets, and black-eyed Susans.

Just .8 mile from the start, after some switchbacks, you'll reach the summit but no view; a trailpost tells you that the elevation here is 2,940 feet. Here you have a right option and a left option. Leave the AT and turn RIGHT here, onto a blue-blazed trail. In .2 mile, after climbing over and around rocks, you'll reach the viewpoint—a series of rocks and ledges with plenty of room for relaxing and plenty of view. The greenish-gray rocks are part of the ancient lava flow which metamorphosed into the greenstone of the Catoctin formation.

You'll see both east—over the Piedmont, and west—over the Shenandoah Valley and some of the bends of the Shenandoah River to Massanutten Mountain. To the right, you'll be looking at the side of Carson Mountain and a stretch of Skyline Drive. This viewspot, surrounded by mountain ash, blueberry bushes, alders, and small oaks, is truly enchanting. Look for some tall gray ghosts—dead trees, killed by gypsy moth caterpillars—a little way down the mountain.

To return to your car, retrace your steps. When you reach the trailpost at the summit, you can choose to take the left option—.2 mile to a limited viewpoint and a large greenstone rock. But this section of trail is rocky and will add 230 feet to your climb.

Pass Mountain

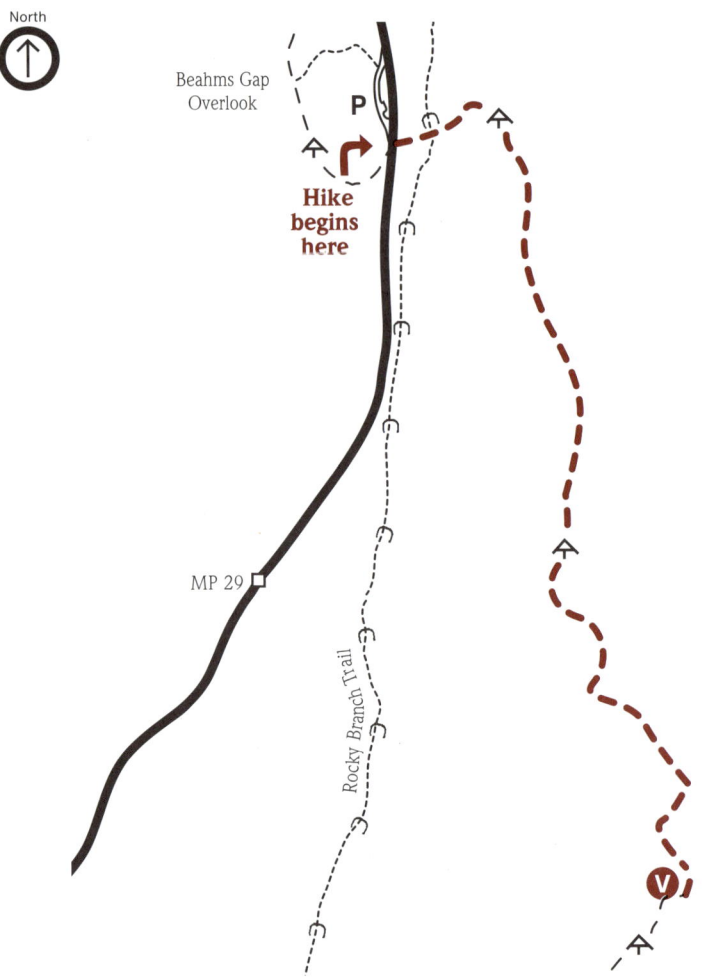

― Legend ―

▬ ▬ ▬	Trail Described	----------	Foot Trail (blue blazes)
▬▬▬	Skyline Drive	MP	Milepost
══════	Access Road	P	Parking
·Ↄ···Ↄ··	Horse Trail (yellow blazes)	V	Viewpoint
– ⌂ –	AT (white blazes)		

Pass Mountain
Skyline Drive access: mile 28.5

A hike up Pass Mountain is a hike through a former homesite and then through one of the park's wilderness areas, and all on the AT. This **round-trip hike** of **1.6 miles** involves a fairly easy climb, and the view you reach is superb.

Park at Beahms Gap Overlook on the west side of the Drive at mile 28.5. Cross the Drive south of the overlook, where the AT crosses, to a trailpost—which gives the miles to various points north and south but doesn't mention the viewspot you're heading for. Start uphill anyway, moving south, and have faith!

Follow the white blazes of the AT. In .1 mile you'll pass another trailpost, where the Rocky Branch Trail crosses. Continue ahead on the AT. This area was once a clearing for a home, so you're in a young, pioneer forest. The trail is open to the sky! You'll see young black locusts and striped maples, along with a few old apple trees, oaks, and hickories. There are grasses, ferns, wildflowers, and lots of butterflies in summer. After half a mile or so, as the trail gets rockier and steeper, you'll be in older forest. Since 1976 this area has been federally designated as wilderness; natural processes are allowed to proceed with only the least possible human interference.

There's no view from the summit of Pass Mountain (3,052 feet); you'll reach the viewpoint before you're all the way to the top. As you near the viewpoint, you'll walk between large boulders. At a huge boulder on the left, just as the trail curves left sharply, turn RIGHT. There's a path. Walk on it to a small ledge; then walk a few steps more to a larger and very craggy ledge (greenstone of the Catoctin formation).

The view is westward, out over Kemp Hollow and the town of Luray, with Neighbor Mountain to the right. You're facing New Market Gap in Massanutten Mountain, with Shenandoah Mountain beyond that. Note the mountain to the left. It's 7 miles away, and it's Stony Man, at 4,010 feet the second highest peak in the park. The ledge you're standing on is sheltered amidst blueberry and blackberry bushes, mountain laurel, and some low oaks.

To return to your starting point, simply retrace your steps.

Marys Rock

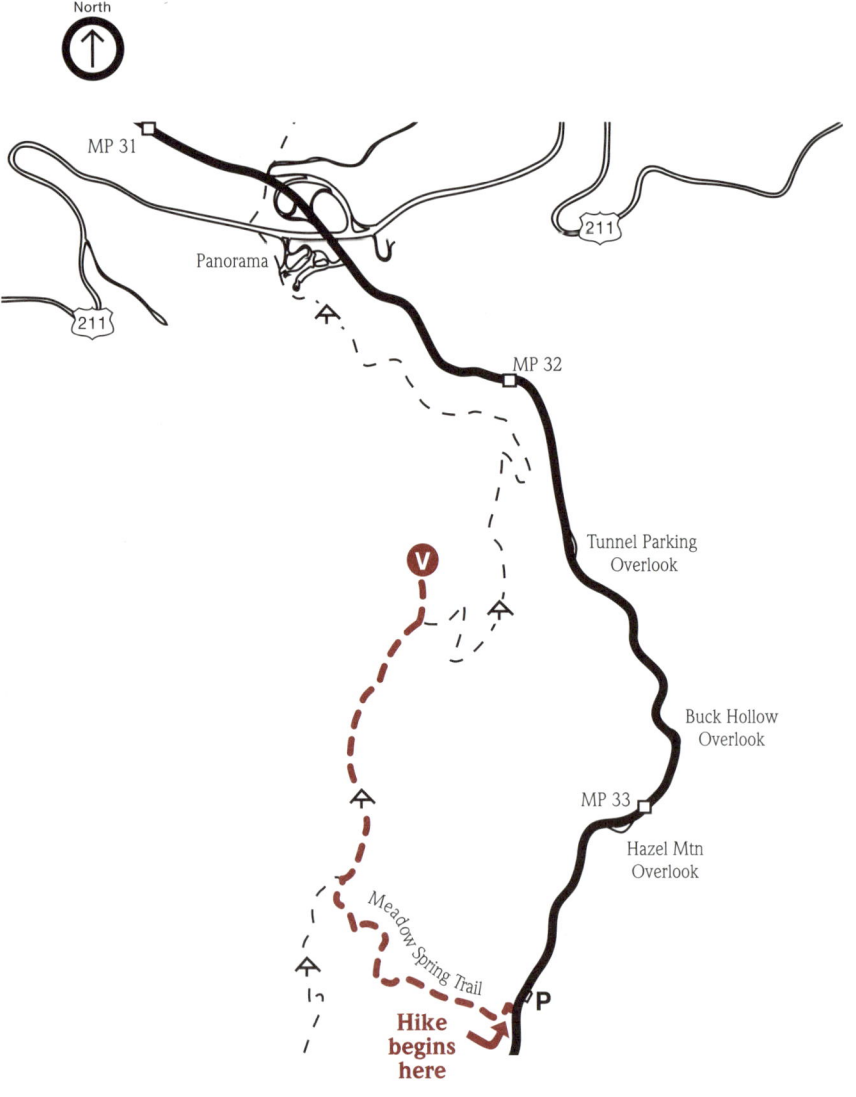

Marys Rock
Skyline Drive access: mile 33.5

Few peaks in the park offer what this one does: a view east across a section of the Piedmont as well as west over the Shenandoah Valley. The **round-trip hike** of **2.8 miles** is sometimes steep, sometimes level, but always exciting.

Park at the Meadow Spring parking area at mile 33.5 on the east side of the Drive. Cross the Drive at the crosswalk and walk a few yards south to a trailpost and the trailhead. Start uphill on the blue-blazed Meadow Spring Trail; it's almost .7 mile to the AT. The trail turns sharply to the left almost immediately.

You're walking through an area burnt in the largest fire in the park's history, October-November, 2000. Charred logs and tree trunks will bear witness to the fire for years to come. But mountain laurel is re-sprouting, ferns grow in abundance, and wildflowers bloomed again in the spring following the fire.

In .4 mile, on a level stretch of trail, you'll pass Meadow Spring on the right, and then, after a sharp right turn, a chimney on the left, all that remains of a cabin formerly maintained by the Potomac Appalachian Trail Club. The cabin burned down in 1946. Soon the trail gets steeper, with rocks on both sides, and eventually reaches the AT. A trailpost informs you that Marys Rock is .6 mile ahead. Turn RIGHT onto the white-blazed AT.

After a climb, you'll again reach a level area, with large rocks and rock ledges overlooking the valley to the west. After you've reached yet another trailpost, turn LEFT onto a blue-blazed trail for .1 mile. When you're on the peak, you'll know it!

What a view! From immense rocks and ledges of the Pedlar Formation (granitic rocks dating back perhaps over a billion years), you can see west over the Shenandoah Valley, partially east over the Piedmont, and straight down to a tiny little Thornton Gap Entrance Station and Panorama. The actual high point up here (3,515 feet) is atop the large rock just behind you.

To return to your car, simply retrace your steps.

There's a longer and steeper **alternate** hike to Marys Rock: take the AT (south) directly behind Panorama. Follow the white blazes steadily uphill, with some switchbacks, then leave the AT for the blue-blazed trail .1 mile from the top. This **round-trip hike** is **3.7 miles** and has a climb of 1,210 feet (instead of 830).

Stony Man Mountain

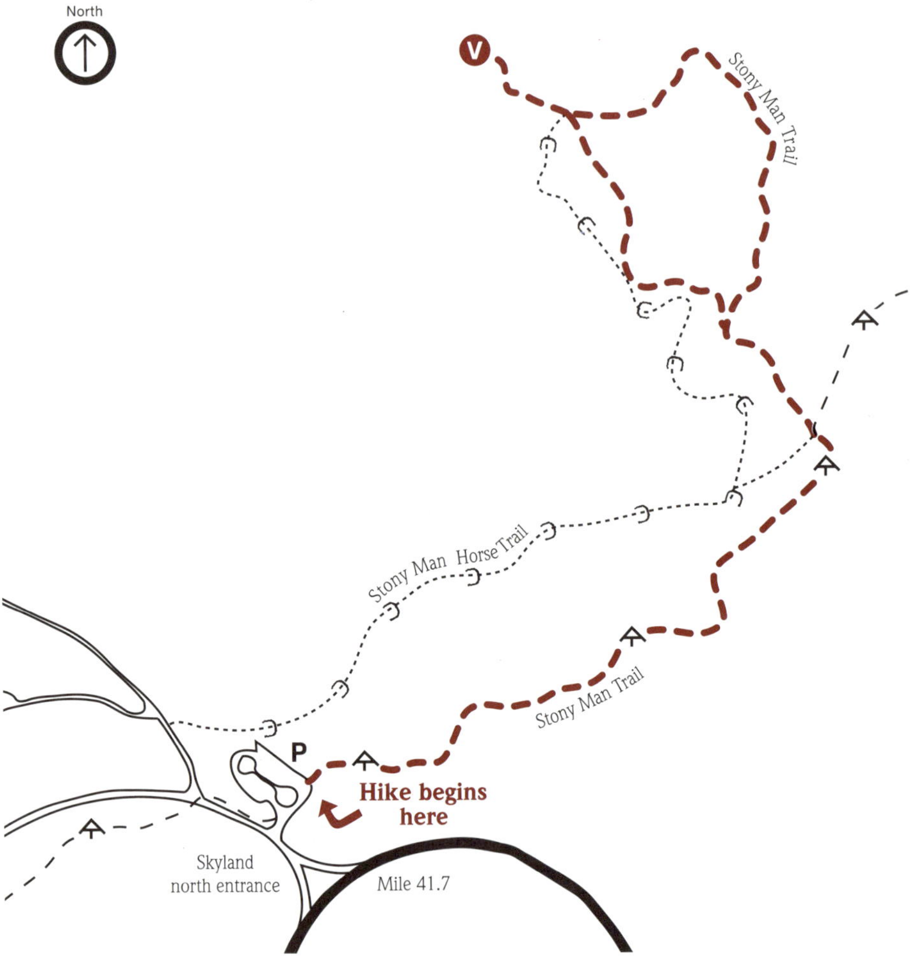

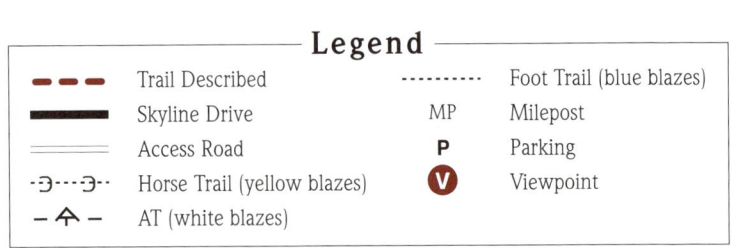

Stony Man Mountain
Skyline Drive access: mile 41.7
Pets are not allowed on this trail.

From Stony Man Overlook, mile 38.6 along Skyline Drive, you can see the profile of his face looking west. But you can climb to his forehead and look west with him! The **round-trip hike** up Stony Man Mountain is only **1.6 miles**, the climb is moderate, and there is beauty all the way, in every season.

Park in the Stony Man parking area, just inside the north entrance to the Skyland area at mile 41.7. The trail begins at the upper right end of the lot. At a dispenser, you may purchase a **guide** to read as you pass numbered posts along the trail.

As you start the hike, you'll be on the AT with its white blazes. The trail begins amidst ferns on both sides. It's not unusual to see a deer or a rabbit in the ferns. The wide trail passes mountain laurel, striped maples, oak and cherry trees, and young chestnuts (which will succumb to the chestnut blight as they mature). Higher up, you'll also pass red spruce and balsam fir, remnants from the last Ice Age. In spring, listen for towhees, scarlet tanagers, warblers, and other birds preparing nests.

When a double blaze warns you that the AT is turning right, don't turn with it. Continue STRAIGHT AHEAD on a blue-blazed trail, amidst young locust trees, birches, and hemlocks. At one point you'll come to a fork in the trail; keep to the RIGHT. Soon you'll have a view of Nicholson Hollow to the east. Then you'll come to a horse hitching rail; turn RIGHT to reach the rocks and the view. You'll be standing on the park's second highest peak (4,010 feet), on rocks which are part of an ancient lava flow later metamorphosed into greenstone.

The view on a clear day is unforgettable: the valley, the town of Luray, Massanutten Mountain, and far, far off—the Alleghenies in West Virginia. The buildings of Skyland lie below to the left; Skyline Drive winds below to the right. If there are clouds, they throw shadows across peaks and ridges.

To return, retrace your steps to the hitching rail. From here walk STRAIGHT AHEAD—don't take the horse trail to the right or the trail to the left. After a short walk you'll join the trail you walked up on. Then retrace your steps to the parking area.

Hawksbill Mountain

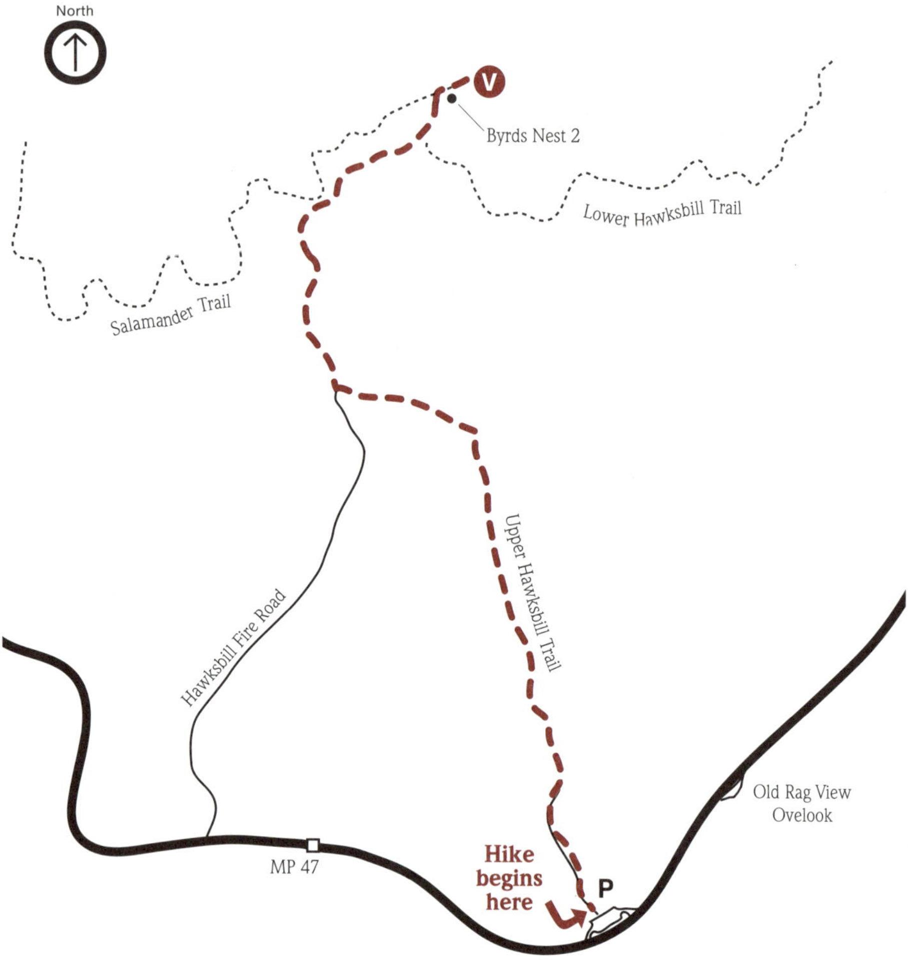

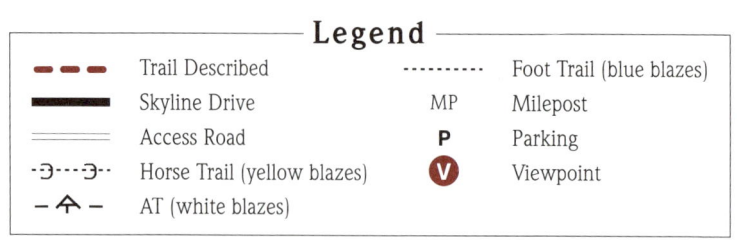

Hawksbill Mountain
Skyline Drive access: mile 46.7

The summit of Hawksbill Mountain (4,050 feet) is the highest point in the park and offers a widespread view to both west and east. The trail to the summit is wide and gentle; the climb on this **round-trip hike** of **2.1 miles** is moderate. There are other routes up Hawksbill, but the one given here is the easiest.

Park your car in the Upper Hawksbill parking area, mile 46.7, on the west side of the Drive. The Upper Hawksbill Trail starts from the back end. Immediately you'll enter woods, on a blue-blazed trail so wide that you hardly need to look for blazes. You'll be in an oak forest—a few old oaks, many young. You'll also see striped maples, hemlocks, and young chestnuts (which the chestnut blight will kill before they mature). Ferns cover the ground on both sides. After .7 mile, a double blaze signals a slight right turn onto Hawksbill Fire Road and a trailpost indicates that the summit is only .3 mile ahead. The trail gets wider now, a little steeper, and also more open, with dead oaks (killed by gypsy moths) on both sides. You'll see sky and sun above.

There's another double blaze and another trailpost .1 mile from the summit. Continue to follow the blue blazes and the fire road. When you reach Byrds Nest 2, a day-use shelter, you're at the top. Turn RIGHT in front of the shelter and walk about 50 yards to the stone observation platform. The platform stands atop greenstone, rock from an ancient lava flow.

This view is magnificent! Skyline Drive winds below to the left. The Shenandoah Valley and Massanutten Mountain lie directly to the west, and on a clear day you can see to the Alleghenies in West Virginia. Then look east: that's Old Rag Mountain, standing ahead of the foothills of the Piedmont. You'll see turkey vultures wheeling and dipping—and they're usually below you! In the fall, look for migrating hawks.

This summit is an achievement, but the walk itself is worth any effort. On warm, sunny days, you'll see butterflies near the fire road and summit. In season, wildflowers color the trailsides: violets, golden ragwort, wild azalea, bluets, and cinquefoil among them. You may meet deer, especially among the ferns.

To return to your car, simply retrace your steps. After leaving the observation platform, be sure to pass Byrds Nest 2 before turning left to move down the mountain.

Hightop Mountain

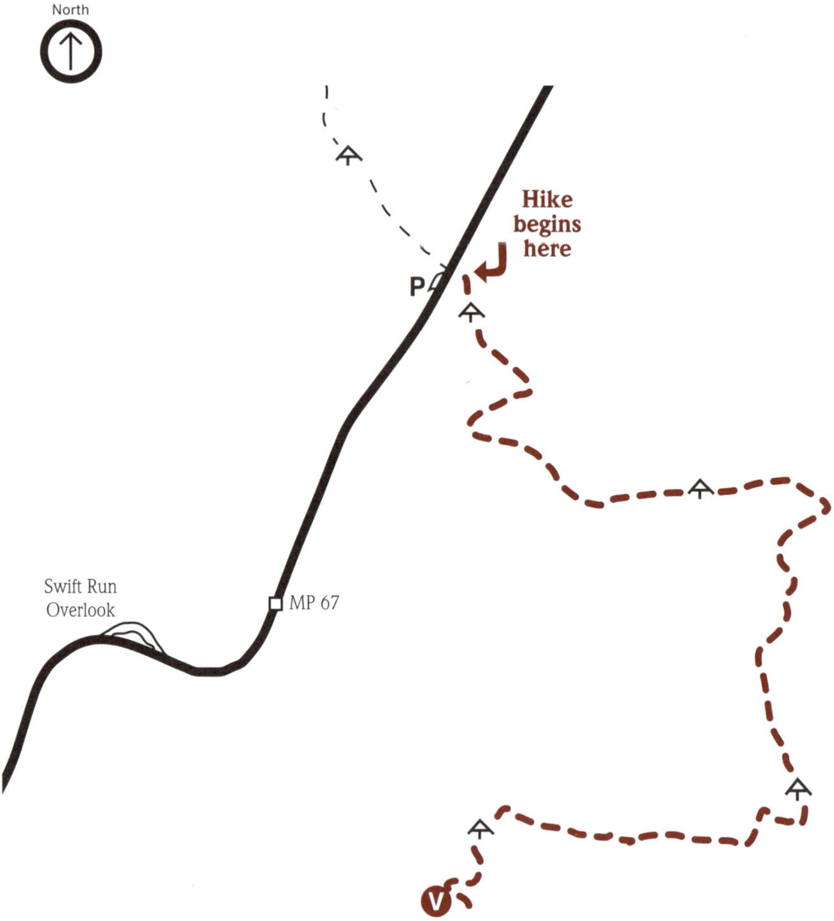

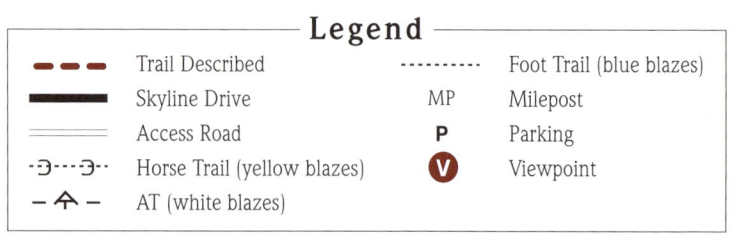

Hightop Mountain
Skyline Drive access: mile 66.7

The view from Hightop Mountain is truly awe-inspiring. Consider this at the outset, because the **round-trip hike** of **3 miles** involves a climb of over 900 feet and you may wonder if the view is worth the effort. It is. The viewspot is just before the summit of the mountain, which at 3,587 feet is the highest peak in the South District of the park.

Park in the small parking area on the west side of the Drive at mile 66.7. Cross the Drive to the AT trailpost on the east side and move up the trail, following white blazes. You'll be on the AT all the way to the top. At first you'll pass through what was once a clearing, with black locusts now taking over. The forest here is open to the sky, though later it closes in. As you move higher on a gentle incline, you'll notice rocks and boulders to both sides, some of them quite beautiful, many with quartz veins. The trail has several switchbacks and some steeper sections as it climbs higher amidst oak trees young and old, cherry trees, and striped maples. About halfway up the trail, you'll come to a felled giant of a tree, knocked down in 1996 by Tropical Storm Fran. At this spot an American redstart once entertained a group of hikers as it flitted from tree to tree.

Hike this trail in May and you'll find trilliums and more trilliums scattered beside the route. Other wildflowers blooming in May include star chickweed, jack-in-the-pulpit, may-apple, meadow rue, wild azalea, wild geranium. There are other flowers in summer and fall, and always lots of ferns.

After 1.5 miles, you'll come to a rock ledge on the right. Don't stay here for long; this ledge offers only a partial view. The prime viewspot is only a few yards on, after the trail has swung left around the summit; turn right onto a short side trail leading to a large, rough ledge with an unblocked and expansive view westward. The mountains to the south are lined up before you, peak after peak. The valley is there also, and Massanutten Mountain, and a tiny overlook on the Drive to the left below—Swift Run Overlook. You'll be standing on the greenstone of the Catoctin formation, the rock found on many of the peaks. It's a greenish-gray rock metamorphosed from an ancient lava flow.

To return to your car, simply retrace your steps.

Loft Mountain

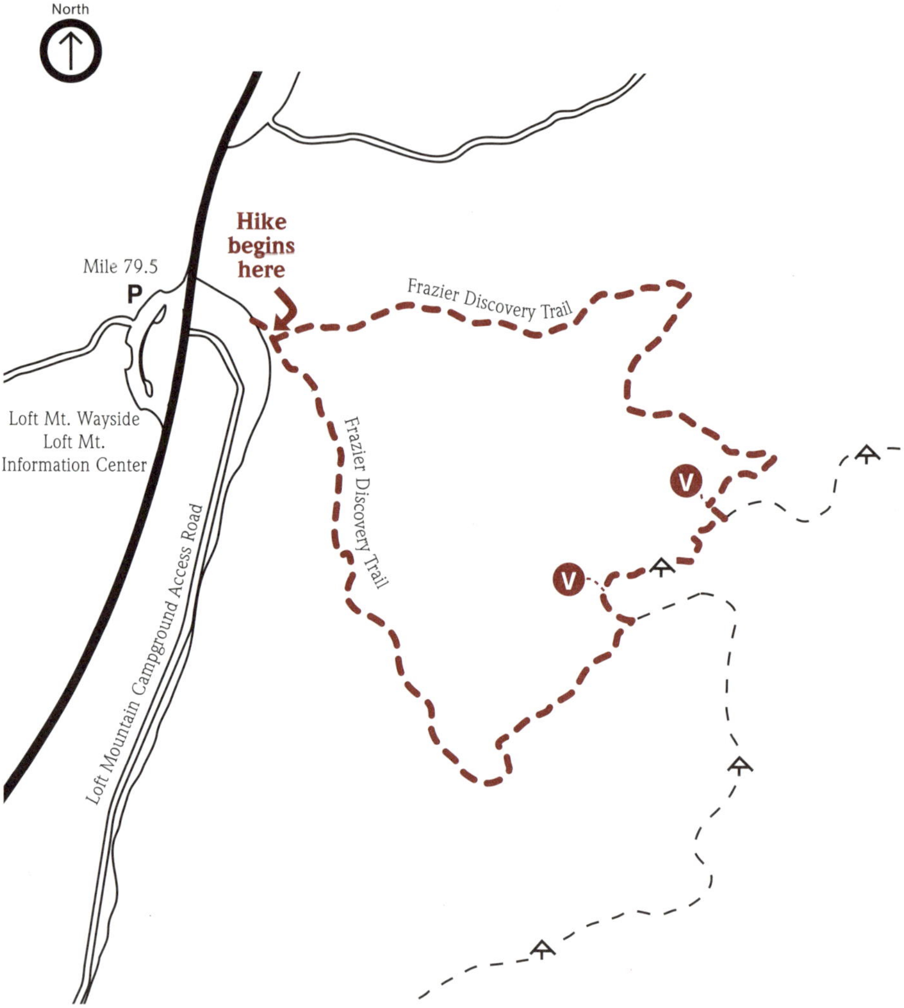

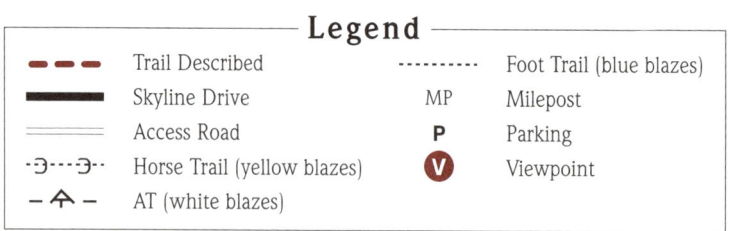

Loft Mountain
Skyline Drive access: mile 79.5
Pets are not allowed on this trail.

The Frazier Discovery Trail on Loft Mountain is a guarantee: you'll enjoy every step of this **circuit hike** of **1.3 miles** as you discover the world of Shenandoah. And no one reaches the viewspot at the top without staying for minutes, or even hours.

Park in the large lot by the Loft Mountain Information Center and the Wayside on the west side of the Drive at mile 79.5. You may purchase an **illustrated guide** at either place or at the trailhead. Cross the Drive at the crosswalk. Go up the paved walkway for 100 yards to a sign directing you to turn left to the trailhead, which is at the bottom of a loop. You may walk in either direction up the mountain on the blue-blazed trail. The trail joins the white-blazed AT at the top for about .1 mile. Read the trailpost directions when you begin your return from the top, so that you descend on the blue-blazed trail and not the AT.

The trail is named after the Frazier family, who years ago lived near here on land belonging to the Pattersons. The south side of the trail loop was once a cleared field; the trees here are young, a pioneer forest beginning to take over. But you'll pass older trees, too, especially on the north side of the trail loop. You'll notice trees knocked down in storms, some of them with tall, upended bases (rootballs). In summer, when you see bushes with berries the color of coral, know that they are appropriately named "coral berry." There are blackberry bushes, too, giving hikers a special treat in late July and August. And wildflowers abound, too many species to list, from the wild geranium of spring and the Queen Anne's lace and wild columbine of summer to fall's purple clematis, spotted jewelweed, and asters.

The rocks along the trail are often covered with lichens and moss. On the north side of the loop, you'll stop at a gigantic overhanging cliff formed from steeply-dipping greenstone, the rock metamorphosed from ancient lava flows. The rocks of this mountain are ancient volcanic rocks, born in tumult.

At the two viewpoints of the summit (3,317 feet), at first you may not notice the rocks, or the hay-scented ferns, or the turkey vultures gliding overhead. Why? Because you'll be gazing to the west—peak after peak, the valley beyond, beyond that the far Alleghenies in West Virginia. You'll sit on the rocks. You'll stay awhile!

Chimney Rock

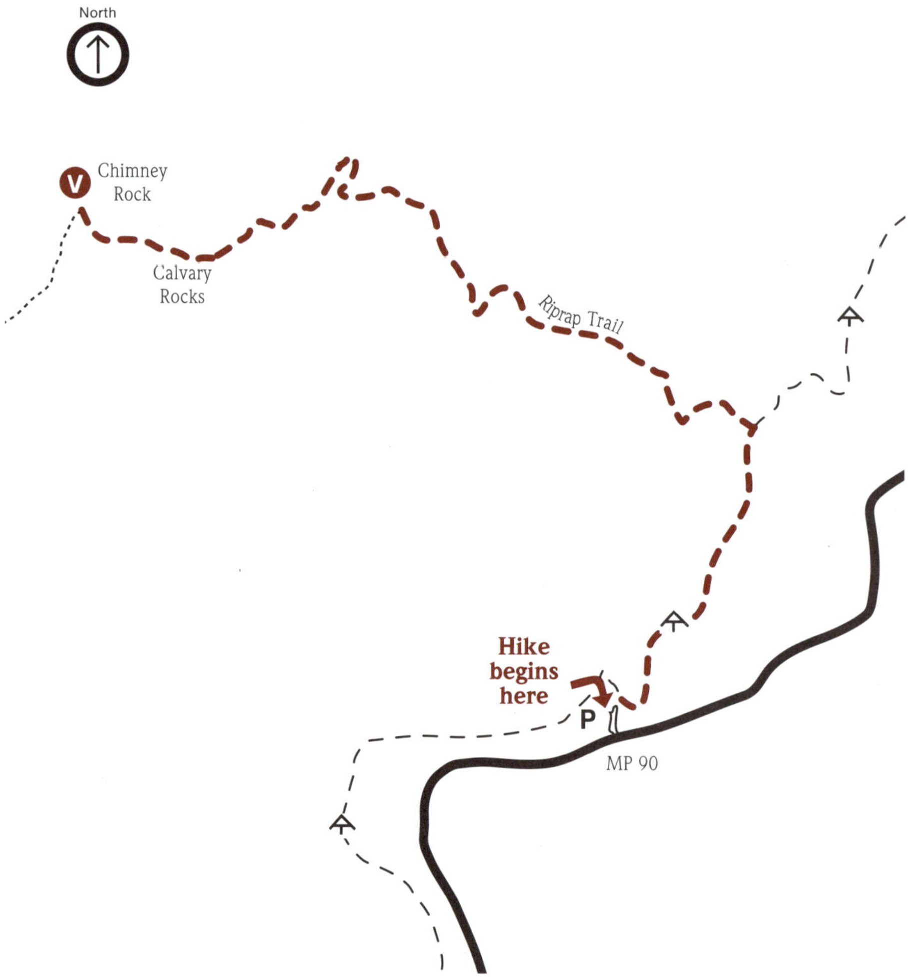

North

- Chimney Rock (V)
- Calvary Rocks
- Riprap Trail
- Hike begins here
- P
- MP 90

Legend

- - -	Trail Described	....	Foot Trail (blue blazes)
▬▬	Skyline Drive	MP	Milepost
═══	Access Road	P	Parking
-Ɔ---Ɔ-	Horse Trail (yellow blazes)	V	Viewpoint
-⋏-	AT (white blazes)		

Chimney Rock
Skyline Drive access: milepost 90

The **round-trip hike** of **3.4 miles** to Chimney Rock, the longest in this guide, may be the most rewarding. You'll ascend and descend through a wilderness area now recovering from two wildfires to a viewspot (2,680 feet) near what is arguably the park's most beautiful rock structure, Chimney Rock.

Park at the Riprap parking area on the west side of the Drive at milepost 90. Begin your hike at the back of the lot. Your entire walk will be through one of the large wilderness areas in the park, designated in 1976 by Congress, to be kept free from human modification. After a few steps, a trailpost and a double blue blaze indicate an intersection with the AT. Turn RIGHT (north) onto the white-blazed AT. The trail here passes some dead trees and charred trunks and limbs on both sides. But there is plenty of green: the area from here to Chimney Rock and beyond is regenerating after the Shop Run Fire (1999) and the Calvary Rocks Fire (1998). Wildflowers growing in abundance tell the story of renewal, including hawkweed, deptford pink, and purple-flowering raspberry. The mountain laurel is resprouting. In August you'll discover ripe blueberries.

After .4 mile, the AT goes straight ahead at a trailpost, but you turn LEFT onto the blue-blazed Riprap Trail. The trail becomes narrower, with some rocky spots and switchbacks. At a right turn, a magnificent talus slope looms—pinkish-white rocks, jagged and angular. Soon you'll pass a viewpoint on the right; stand on the large, pinkish blocks to look north over the Paine Run watershed. Note the long, thin skolithos tubes in the rocks—the fossilized burrows of worms in an ancient ocean (over 500 million years ago). Then the trail goes down and up through dense forest. You'll pass beautiful white cliffs on the left: Calvary Rocks. Then it's up and down again for .2 mile.

At a sharp left turn, move right—to see a spectacular wall-like block of white rock beyond a deep vertical cleft: Chimney Rock. You'll notice steel spikes in the rock, where a footbridge spanned the chasm before this became a wilderness area. This rock and those along the trail are quartzite outcrops of the Erwin formation (metamorphosed sandstone). You can gaze beyond the rock—across the Paine Run watershed to the beauty of the surrounding peaks.

To return to your car, simply retrace your steps.

Turk Mountain

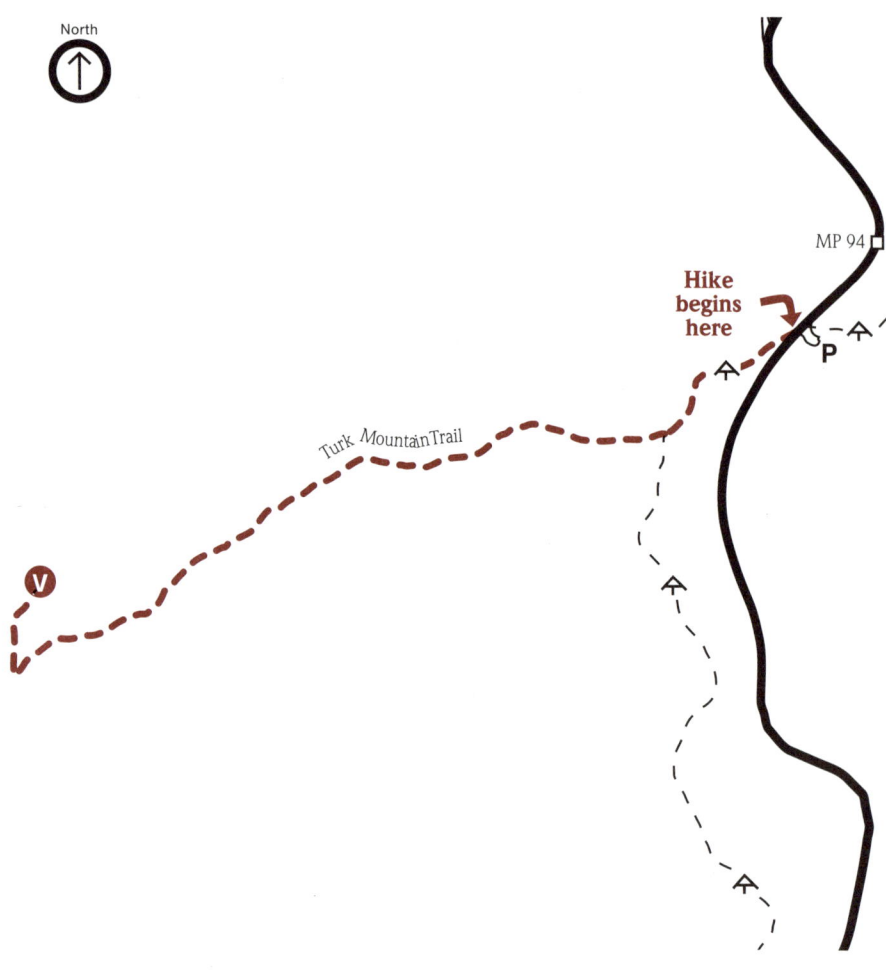

Turk Mountain
Skyline Drive access: mile 94.1

The **round-trip hike** of **2.2 miles** to the top of Turk Mountain is popular, and rightly so. Until the end, the climb is gradual, in the deep forest of one of the park's wilderness areas. You'll cross a very interesting talus slope before you reach the summit and its impressive view.

Park in the parking area on the east side of the Drive at mile 94.1. Cross the Drive to the AT trailpost on the west side; the trailpost tells you that Turk Mountain Summit is 1.1 miles ahead. Start downhill on the AT, following the white blazes. Then you'll move gradually uphill in deep shade on a trail that's not rocky. At another trailpost, the AT turns left. Go STRAIGHT AHEAD on the blue-blazed Turk Mountain Trail.

You'll walk down into the saddle of the mountain, then up again; the trail will become more rocky. Soon after leaving the AT you'll enter a wilderness area, land designated by Congress in 1976 to be kept free from human interference. You're walking in a mixed forest, including oaks, maples, and sassafras, a few pines, with lots of mountain laurel. You'll find blueberry bushes, too, mosses and ferns, and wildflowers—like hawkweed, long-leaved bluets, coreopsis, and Indian cucumber root.

Toward the top of the mountain you'll walk over a talus slope of Erwin quartzite (metamorphosed sandstone). You might enjoy studying individual rocks here: skolithos tubes are preserved within the pinkish-white quartzites, and you can find them! These tubes are the fossilized burrows of ancient worms (from the early to middle Cambrian time period, over 500 million years ago). If the rock surface is cut perpendicular to the bedding, you'll see the long, thin tubes vertically; if the rock cut is parallel to the bedding, you'll see small circles (2-3 mm in diameter). Be sure to leave these fascinating rocks where you find them.

Then you'll climb steeply uphill, over switchbacks, to the summit (2,981 feet). You'll be standing at the top of the talus slope, on immense, pinkish-white Erwin quartzite rocks, looking far north and west. You're likely to find other hikers sitting on the rocks: this place is hard to leave!

Simply retrace your steps to return to your car. Remember to go straight ahead onto the AT when you reach it.

If You Want More...

These hikes may whet your appetite for other adventures in Shenandoah National Park. Rangers will be happy to advise you about hikes at the Dickey Ridge Visitor Center (mile 4.6), the Harry F. Byrd, Sr. Visitor Center (milepost 51), and the Loft Mountain Information Center (mile 79.5). At visitor centers and at park concession facilities, you can purchase maps and guides. Here are a few.

- *PATC Map #9, North District*, Potomac Appalachian Trail Club
- *PATC Map #10, Central District*, Potomac Appalachian Trail Club
- *PATC Map #11, South District*, Potomac Appalachian Trail Club
- *Shenandoah National Park Topo Map*, National Geographic
- *Short Hikes in Shenandoah National Park*, Joanne Amberson, Shenandoah National Park Association
- *Circuit Hikes in Shenandoah National Park*, Potomac Appalachian Trail Club
- *Hiking Shenandoah National Park*, Bert and Jane Gildart, Globe Pequot Press
- *Easy Hikes on the Appalachian National Scenic Trail in Shenandoah National Park*, Joanne Amberson, Shenandoah National Park Association
- *75 Hikes in Virginia's Shenandoah National Park*, Russ Manning, The Mountaineers
- *PATC Appalachian Trail Guide #7*, Potomac Appalachian Trail Club
- *Hikes to Waterfalls in Shenandoah National Park*, Joanne Amberson, Shenandoah National Park Association

You can order these and many other books and maps anytime from the Shenandoah National Park Association (SNPA), a nonprofit educational organization supporting the interpretive and educational activities of Shenandoah National Park. Profits from sales of all items are used to support these activities. For further information about SNPA and a list of publications available for purchase, contact:

Shenandoah National Park Association
3655 US Hwy 211 E., Luray, VA 22835
(540) 999-3582
website: www.snpbooks.org